EVANGELISTIC
PRAYER

Engaging the Power of God for the Lost

DR. J. KIE BOWMAN

PRAYERSHOP
PUBLISHING

Terre Haute, Indiana

PrayerShop Publishing is the publishing arm of the Church Prayer Leaders Network.

The Church Prayer Leaders Network exists to equip and inspire local churches and prayer leaders in their desire to disciple people in prayer and to become a "house of prayer for all nations." Its online store, prayershop.org, offers more than 150 prayer resources for purchase or download.

ISBN (Print): 978-1-970176-33-9
ISBN (E-Book): 978-1-970176-34-6

Scripture quotations are from The ESV® Bible (The Holy Bible, English Standard Version®), © 2001 by Crossway, a publishing ministry of Good News Publishers. Used by permission. All rights reserved.

Printed in the United States of America

DEDICATION

I dedicate this book to the congregation of
Hyde Park Baptist Church in Austin, Texas, where I served as
Senior Pastor for more than 25 years.

Together we prayed thousands into the Kingdom.

ACKNOWLEDGMENTS

There are many people to thank because a book is never a solitary project. First, I want to thank my friend Jonathan Graf from PrayerShop Publshing for recruiting me to write this project. I first became familiar with Jon more than 20 years ago by reading one of his books on prayer. Later, in various encounters, through our mutual commitment to the prayer movement, we became friends. Eventually, he became my publisher, with this being my second book with PrayerShop, and hopefully not my last.

I also want to thank Blair Hodges, my former Executive Assistant at Hyde Park Baptist Church, for his editorial and secretarial assistance on this book. When I accepted this writing assignment, I had already decided to retire as Senior Pastor. By the time I had completed it, I had retired and was Senior Pastor Emeritus, which meant Blair was no longer my assistant. Still, on his own time, he was willing to continue his valuable editorial and grammatical reviews. Obviously, any mistakes are mine, but I'm confident there are far fewer than there would have been as a result of Blair's keen eye and knowledge of grammar and style.

As always, I want to thank my wife, Tina. We went through a major transition this year as I was retiring, completing the manuscript, and moving my writing to our home. She has always lived with my writing projects more than anyone else, but this one intensified while I finished in my home office. She was patient and encouraging and, fortunately, understands me like no one else. I thank God for her.

Of course, I want to thank Hyde Park Baptist Church, where many of these principles were practiced for more than a quarter of a century. We started on a journey together years ago to be a "house of prayer" while winning as many people to the Lord as possible. They are great people.

Finally, a book is much more than whatever the author is thinking about at the moment. A lifetime of consideration about prayer and evangelism, and evangelistic prayer, has culminated in this work. As a result of thinking about these subjects and practicing these disciplines for more than 45 years, I have naturally read a lot, heard a lot, and been exposed to a lot that has influenced my thinking. When you have lived with an obsession for nearly 50 years, it's hard to remember how you came upon some of your own thoughts. When writing, however, it is important to give credit to the work of previous and current authors whose work you rely upon. I have endeavored to do that wherever possible. Still, the influence of multiple generations of writers, evangelists, and teachers is, no doubt, reflected in my thought process and, in some cases, perhaps even my words. I owe them all a great debt because often their thinking has become my thinking. Any uncredited similarities to other works are unintentional, and every effort has been made to properly acknowledge dependence where required.

J. Kie Bowman
Austin, Texas

TABLE OF CONTENTS

INTRODUCTION

How to Use This Book

When Jonathan Graf, Publisher at PrayerShop Publishing, asked me to write this book, I jumped at the chance.

Early on, I decided to follow Scripture by only writing about those passages which directly mention prayer and also impact the advancement of the gospel.

We agreed this would be a short book, so I have included eight major passages, and thus we have eight fairly short chapters. There are other passages I might have included, but for what we were trying to do, I covered the necessary material.

At the end of chapters 2-8 there are sections called "Prayer Prompts" and "My Prayer Lists." The idea is for each reader to turn the information learned from the chapter into a personal prayer guide.

Suggestions for Reading

This book is designed to increase the practice of prayer and help you become more effective in prayer evangelism.

- Read this book with a highlighter and a pen in hand. Read and think through a chapter a day.
- Identify the people you want to pray for.
- Use the prayer prompts at the end of every chapter as your prayer guide for the day.

Eventually, these suggestions for how to pray more evangelistically will become an instinctive part of your daily prayer habit.

Finally, after you have become familiar with the teachings of the book and the prayer prompts, you should consider teaching this book to small groups in your church. Organize a home Bible study or a prayer group at your office or dorm. Share what you've learned so that more people pray, and more people come to know Christ through prayer evangelism.

CHAPTER 1

The Acts Blueprint

Your culture will determine your future. Every family, every business, every church, and every people group united by a common ideology has an individual culture—the unique fingerprint of that group. I agree with business expert Peter Drucker, who was probably the first to say, "Culture eats strategy for breakfast."

Nowhere is the culture more important to an organization than in the hiring of the people who make up the workforce. As the lead pastor of a large church with a large staff, I conducted hundreds of interviews over the years. Building a team with the right DNA was always a top priority. We obviously wanted people with competence and character but also people who could flourish within our culture.

Since the right fit is crucial early in the hiring process, we wanted future team members to understand our staff culture. Two of our consistent team values were evangelism and prayer. One day I was interviewing a highly competent potential staff member for a key position, and I shared with him about our team values.

His response was both transparent and a little surprising. He half-jokingly said, "Oh great, evangelism and prayer—the two things nobody's good at." We all laughed at his candor, but I've thought a lot about his response.

After spending my entire adult life in ministry and observing how ministers and church members live the Christian life, I think the staff candidate had a point. I've known a few people who were passionate and committed to both evangelism and prayer, but too few. A glance at the state of the American church tells the uncomfortable story.

For instance, a Christian journalist recently reported that a majority of Christians never explain the gospel to a lost person or even invite a friend to church.[1] Even more concerning is the fact that about half of Millennial Christians think evangelism is wrong![2] Obviously, Christianity has spread around the world for 2000 years, becoming the world's largest religion through the faithfulness and, at times, sacrificial evangelism of Christian people. Today, for some in the Body of Christ, however, the legitimacy of sharing our faith appears to be in question, reminding us that Christianity is always only one generation away from extinction.

How should we react to the dramatic downturn in evangelistic fervor and effectiveness? Can this trend be reversed? Yes. We can be much more effective in evangelism. The answer to reigniting the evangelistic passion we need is astoundingly simple,

---

1. Hallowell, Billy. "5 Deeply Concerning Revelations about the State of Christian Evangelism in America." CBN, May 29, 2022. https://www2.cbn.com/news/news/5-deeply-concerning-revelations-about-state-christian-evangelism-america.
2. Shellnutt, Kate. "Half of Millennial Christians Say It's Wrong to Evangelize." News & Reporting, February 6, 2019. https://www.christianitytoday.com/news/2019/february/half-of-millennial-christians-wrong-to-evangelize-barna.html.

but it requires action. Are you ready to take a step and make a difference? Are you ready to understand the relationship between prayer and evangelism?

Unexpected Advice

Jesus said, "Wait." Admittedly, that advice is counterintuitive. After all, didn't Jesus say we should go into all the world? Yes, Jesus said, "go" (Matthew 28:19). But before we "go," Jesus said we should "stop" (Luke 24:49).

The waiting period Jesus referred to is mentioned in the last chapter of Luke and similarly in the first chapter of Acts. The two passages are both written by Luke and clearly reflect the same ideas.

> *"And behold, I am sending the promise of my Father upon you. But stay in the city until you are clothed with power from on high."* (Luke 24:49)

> *"And while staying with them, he ordered them not to depart from Jerusalem, but to wait for the promise of the Father, which, he said, 'You heard from me; for John baptized with water, but you will be baptized with the Holy Spirit not many days from now.'"* (Acts 1:4-5)

It's clear that Jesus wanted His followers to experience the empowering of the Holy Spirit prior to any evangelistic outreach. In many ways, the Apostles, after the resurrection, were the most prepared, knowledgeable, and eager group of people who have ever existed to do mission work. They had first-hand personal knowledge of everything Jesus had done and said during His earthly ministry. In addition, they were eyewitnesses of the cross and the resurrection. They must have been eager to tell their story, but Jesus said they weren't ready. They needed the power of the Holy Spirit. So, He told them to wait in Jerusalem for the outpouring of the Spirit.

We will take up the all-important subject of the Holy Spirit in an in-depth way later, but for our purposes now, I invite you to direct your focus to the idea of waiting. Luke wrote both of these passages, and while they are similar, they do not appear to be part of the same conversation. Or, if they are from the same conversation, they appear to be spoken at different times in the conversation and in slightly different contexts. In other words, Jesus mentioned this more than once.

In these two separate passages, Luke uses two completely different words to describe the waiting process. In Luke's gospel, the word "stay" is used nearly 50 times in the Greek New Testament. It means to sit down or be set in a place. The verb includes the idea of permanence as opposed to momentarily stopping or being set down briefly.

In Acts, however, Luke uses a different word, translated as "wait" (1:4). The word is found only once in the Greek New Testament. It literally means to circle around a place—almost like the idea of hovering. We might even paraphrase it, in a colloquial manner of speaking, as "to hang around."

The most important question related to these two words is this—how did the Apostles interpret Jesus' instructions when He told them to stay or wait? How did they imagine "waiting"? How did they wait? They prayed.

In Luke's gospel, we're told they went to the Temple "continually" to praise God (Luke 24:52). In Acts, we find them praying in the large upper room of a home (Acts 1:14). For ten days, therefore, from the Ascension of Jesus until Pentecost, we find the followers of Christ doing nothing but splitting their time between praising God publicly at the Temple and praying privately together in the upper room. In answer to their non-stop prayer meetings, God fulfilled the promise of Jesus and poured out the Holy Spirit onto the praying church.

The Acts Blueprint

Within minutes after the Spirit filled them, the disciples were out of the house, into the street, and preaching the first sermon of the Church! The result was phenomenal. That day 3,000 people gave their lives to Christ and were baptized (Acts 2:41).

Have you ever wondered how many people were saved between the Resurrection and Pentecost? None are recorded. Think about that. The Apostles spent about three years with Jesus and apparently did not reproduce themselves even one time in 50 days, with all of the knowledge, information, and personal experience available to them. But after the 10-day prayer meeting and the coming of the Spirit, 3,000 were saved and baptized. Does that suggest anything to us? It should.

Immediately after the baptism of 3,000 people, the church organized itself into a teaching, loving, praying community (Acts 2:42). When Luke summarized those idyllic early days, he said they were, *"praising God and having favor with all the people. And the Lord added to their number day by day those who were being saved"* (Acts 2:47). They prayed, and people were saved. It's a pattern Luke will emphasize throughout the book of Acts.

Later when the church was threatened for preaching in Jesus' name, they met again for prayer, and the result of their prayer meeting was bold evangelism (Acts 4:31). When the Church was handicapped by internal divisions, the Apostles encouraged others to address the divisions while they recommitted themselves to prayer and ministering the Word (Acts 6:4). As a result, the ministry of evangelism increased, and even Jewish priests came to Christ in record numbers (Acts 6:7).

When Peter went to Joppa, known today as Tel-Aviv, he prayed for a dead woman who came back to life. The result was an evangelistic flurry in the city, and "many believed in the Lord" (Acts 9:40-42).

Then, years later, in the city of Antioch, now in modern-day Turkey, a group of five leaders gathered for a prayer meeting. While they were fasting and praying, the Holy Spirit called Barnabas and Saul (Paul) to evangelize the Gentiles (Acts 13:1-5). This became the biggest of all evangelistic enterprises because it took the gospel outside of a small, exclusive focus on Jews and out to the rest of the world.

What have we noticed in this overview of evangelism in the book of Acts? For one thing, prayer preceded every evangelistic outreach mentioned. Fortunately for us, the Acts pattern of prayer and evangelistic success is not limited to the pages of the Bible. The pattern has proven true wherever people have prayed for more souls to turn to Christ.

For instance, in the area of today's financial district in lower Manhattan in New York City, near where the World Trade Center once stood, God worked a miracle more than 150 years ago. The Old North Dutch Church on Fulton Street was more than 100 years old and dying. Its once influential ministry had dwindled to a handful of the faithful. The area around the church had dramatically changed from residential to commercial. Other churches were relocating, but the leadership of the Old North Dutch Church decided to try something new to reach people. They hired a committed Christian businessman to reinvigorate the outreach of the old church. Jeremiah Lanphier started in July and tried a number of things, including going door to door to speak to business leaders, encouraging hotels to send their guests to the nearby church on Sundays, and numerous other efforts without success.

He finally felt so discouraged he decided to host a prayer meeting for the other businessmen in the area. He printed thousands of flyers advertising the noon event, which he handed out on the streets. On September 23, 1857, no one showed up until 12:30. Eventually, that day, six men dropped by to pray. It was an inauspicious beginning, but what happened over the next few weeks was miraculous. The noon prayer meeting eventually started meeting every day, and more people started attending. A financial crisis in New York City drove even more anxious businesspeople to the daily prayer meetings. Within three months, the prayer meetings had spread all over the city and were reaching 50,000 people. Soon, prayer meetings sprang up all over the nation. It was a genuine move of God. Miraculously, 1 million people were saved in 18 months when the U.S. population was only 30 million.[3] The Prayer Revival of 1857-1858 may be the largest evangelistic harvest per capita in U.S. history. How did it happen? The church recognized the need. They found the right leader, and he led prayer meetings, and God saved hundreds of thousands of people.

The Acts blueprint has repeatedly shown itself to be God's desired path for evangelistic harvest wherever it has been attempted. God's people pray, and more people get saved.

Here's a more recent example. Most of us have heard of Jim Cymbala, the pastor of Brooklyn Tabernacle and author of *Fresh Wind, Fresh Fire*. A few years ago, Pastor Cymbala came to my church in Austin to train a small group of pastors. He talked about

---

3. Barrick, Audrey. "Christians Mark 150 Years of Fulton Street Revival." The Christian Post, September 23, 2007. https://www.christianpost.com/news/christians -mark-150-years-of-fulton-street-revival.html.

God's call for him to lead Brooklyn Tabernacle to prioritize prayer. Today the Tuesday night prayer meeting attracts not only several thousand people from his congregation but also people from around the world who want to experience what God has done in Brooklyn. I'm one of them. I've attended the Tuesday night prayer meeting several times.

For our small group of pastors in Austin, Cymbala warned us not to assume we would all have 3,000 people at our prayer meetings right away. He wisely cautioned us to start in faith, even if we started small. He then explained that the first prayer meeting after he started leading his church to pray consisted of a little more than a dozen people who stood in a circle holding hands. They prayed everything they could think of in five minutes. That was it. It's humorous when you think about what it eventually became.

One of the most amazing testimonies of the last 30 years in the Body of Christ has been the miracle of the Brooklyn Tabernacle Tuesday night prayer meeting, but it started in an awkward, normal, unimpressive way. The key to the growth of the prayer meeting and of the church was what followed. According to Pastor Cymbala, the little group of prayer warriors started seeing people on their prayer lists getting saved. A wayward son here, a disinterested husband there, and eventually, the miracles of salvation became too numerous to ignore. God's people prayed, and lost people got saved. The church grew to an attendance of more than 10,000 with conversion testimonies that have inspired the Body of Christ for decades.

The Acts blueprint worked in first-century Jerusalem, in 19th-century Manhattan, and in 20th-century Brooklyn. It works wherever it's tried. Unfortunately, we often don't step out in faith to try it. As F. B. Meyer once observed, "The greatest tragedy of life is not unanswered prayer but unoffered prayer."

Will you pray for more people to be saved? Will you pray evangelistic prayers?

In the following pages, we will review some of the greatest verses of Scripture on the subject of prayer and evangelism. At the end of each chapter, you'll find "prayer prompts" suggesting practical ways for you to incorporate the kind of prayer for evangelism mentioned in the New Testament. The goal of this book is the expansion of the Kingdom of God through a recommitment to prayer for the fulfillment of the Great Commission. All of us can make this commitment if we will.

CHAPTER 2

Praying Like
You Mean It!

*"Brothers, my heart's desire and prayer to God for
them is that they may be saved."* —Romans 10:1

Is it possible to be bored in the 21st century? Surprisingly, in spite
of having access to multiple streaming services for movies and
music, near-universal access to the internet, and the beauty of the
great outdoors, a recent survey finds that Americans spend one-
third of their time bored.[4] Boredom might be hard for some of us
to relate to, but we can all agree that nothing zaps the life out of us
like boredom.

---

4. When Monotony Strikes Average American. https://www.dailymail.co.uk/news
/article-7006523/When-monotony-strikes-average-American-spends-131-DAYS
-year-mired-boredom.html/.

None of us wants to live our lives apathetically—just "going through the motions." Isn't it true that we want to live with energy, joy, passion, and purpose? Most of us want lives that matter.

As believers, living with a sense of meaning goes beyond how we spend our free time or what we do on the job. A need for purpose, something to be passionate about, the extra spark that gets us out of bed in the morning with enthusiasm, extends to our spiritual lives as well. In fact, real purpose begins with our spiritual lives. What could be worse, therefore, than a feeling of meaninglessness in prayer?

The Scripture makes it clear that God loves it when His people pray with passion. Jacob, for example, received the blessing when he wrestled with the Angel of the Lord and refused to let go until he was blessed (Genesis 32:24-29). Hannah prayed with such intensity before she received her answer that the priest thought she was drunk (I Samuel 1:12-17). Jesus sweat drops of blood when He prayed in the Garden of Gethsemane (Like 22:44). These three examples are only a sampling of the number of times people in Scripture prayed with passion, intensity, and deep emotion. Praying with passion is biblical.

In numerous instances, God rewarded people who gave themselves without reservation to the ministry of prayer. Fortunately, God hasn't changed. Greg Laurie recently commented on passion in prayer, saying, "Jesus is calling us to passionate, persistent prayer. I think many of our prayers have no power in them because there's no heart in them. And if we put so little heart into our prayers, then we can't expect God to put much heart into answering them."[5]

---

5. Laurie, Greg, and Harvest. "A Call to Passionate, Persistent Prayer." Harvest, August 28, 2020. https://harvest.org/resources/gregs-blog/post/a-call-to-passionate -persistent-prayer/.

The Apostle Paul was passionate about most things- including interceding in prayer for the lost. In speaking about his family members, friends, and members of his previous religion, he said, *"Brothers, my heart's desire and prayer to God for them is that they may be saved"* (Romans 10:1).

Paul put his heart into prayer! Rather than praying in some cool, dispassionate way, he shows us how to "desire" the salvation of the lost. The word translated "desire" comes from a Greek word indicating when a thing is attractive or good—in other words, desirable. For Paul, seeing more people follow Christ "seemed good." The salvation of the lost was the desired outcome of prayer!

His passion for people to be saved challenges the way we pray. Do we care enough to pray with the desire for people to come to Christ? At the core of this kind of prayer, Paul was not advocating mere emotion, although we shouldn't fear genuinely emotional prayers either. Instead, Paul was admitting that he cared deeply for his lost friends, and that concern and love moved him to pray. The prayer streamed not just from a religious duty but from his heart. He loved the people he was praying for. He was like Jesus, who wept over the lostness of Jerusalem. The Lord passionately compared Himself to a parent gathering His children to Himself for their safety and well-being. Can we love our non-Christian unbelieving friends, co-workers, and family members enough to pray like that? Is it even possible for anyone to pray with that kind of passion?

A Heart That Cares

A man of prayer who has profoundly affected millions of people, including myself, is Dick Eastman. He is the immediate past president of Every Home for Christ, a ministry that has reached more than 250 million people for Christ around the world. His life is consumed with prayer and evangelism. His books on prayer have been some of the most influential of the late 20th century and up to this moment. As of this writing, he currently serves as the president of America's National Prayer Committee. His training seminar on prayer has been attended by more than 2 million people. He is an inspirational leader.

As a young minister, Eastman was a youth pastor in California with an unusual burden for prayer. He frequently led his youth group to go on prayer retreats in the mountains of Northern California. On one of those prayer retreats, his group was praying in a lodge at a campground in the beautiful California Redwood Forest. It was 3 o'clock in the morning, and young people were pouring their hearts out to God, praying for the lost to be saved. As the teenagers prayed, Eastman silently asked himself a question. "Why do I feel absolutely no emotion when so many people are dying and going into eternity this very moment without knowing Christ? Why don't I care more for the lost? Please, God," he prayed, "help me care!"

In the next few moments, tears formed in his eyes and started rolling down his face. Soon the tears were uncontrollable, and he began weeping and sobbing with a vision of lost people without Christ. For several hours he cried and prayed until he was filled with peace. Then, he felt as if the Holy Spirit spoke to his heart and said, "Your ministry, for the future, has been born tonight."

Few leaders have been as influential in the body of Christ in our lifetimes as Dick Eastman. His focus on prayer and evangelism has rarely been matched by anyone. And it all started with a prayer, "Help me care."[6] People have come to Christ around the world because of that one prayer.

---

6. Eastman, Dick. *The Purple Pig and Other Miracles*. Page 55-57. Lake Mary, FL: Charisma House, 2011.

Eastman asked himself a question regarding his own relative indifference to people coming to Christ. It was only when he asked God to give him a real concern that the floods of spiritual passion started to flow. Praying *with* a burden for the lost may begin by praying *for* a burden for the lost.

As you pray for your lost friends, family members, and others, can you begin by looking at your own heart? Ask God to give you a burden—a deeply personal longing for other people to be saved. Let your prayers be marked with a passion so that you can honestly say, "My heart's desire is that they may be saved."

Prayer Prompts

- Ask God to give you a burden—a deep personal concern for people who need Jesus.
- Pray with a heart of love and mercy for the person. Ask God to remove from your prayers a judgmental spirit about the wrongs they've done and give you instead heartfelt compassion for their need.
- Pray for them to be forgiven and saved.

My Prayer List

List the people you are praying for and pray for them using the prompts above.

_____

_____

_____

CHAPTER 3

Praying with an Evangelistic Focus

"Brothers, my heart's desire and prayer to God for them is that they may be saved." Romans 10:1

As a speaker, I sometimes use a "laser pointer" to draw attention to small details on the screen, like those features found on a map or in a photograph. Laser pointers are generally inexpensive, but the cheap kind doesn't always have enough intensity to reach the screen with brightness and clarity, especially when the powerful "house lights" are on and the projector lights are bright.

So, a few years ago, I spent ten times more than the normal price of a common laser pointer to buy the brightest beam I had ever seen. It shoots a piercing, intense green light. The first time I used it in church, I was worried some of the members might think I was trying to blind the congregation simply by pointing that incredibly bright green beam at the map on the screen! In other words, it worked almost too well. We were all seeing spots for a few minutes.

Have you wondered what makes a laser light work as it does? Why is it so much brighter than lights like the light bulbs in our house? The difference is the focus. Incandescent light, like that emitted from light bulbs, bathes an entire room in light. A laser, by contrast, is forced into a tightly focused beam. A light bulb in my house might be 60 or 75 watts, and that wattage emits a soft light appropriate for a normal life. Maybe I will even need up to 100 watts for reading. The beam of a laser, on the other hand, which could potentially cause eye damage if one stared into it, has actually a very low wattage. In fact, a blindingly intense laser pointer might be emitting only a single watt! The difference in intensity is not in the wattage—it's in the focus. Laser light harnesses all of its energy into a single beam, and the result is spectacular.

What if we applied the principle of harnessing power into a tight focus in a spiritual sense? When you pray for the lost, for instance, is your prayer life an incandescent bulb or a laser pointer? The difference is all in the focus.

When Paul described his prayer for his friends, he was clear about his focus. He prayed they would be saved (Romans 10:1). Praying for the lost to be saved may seem self-evident, but perhaps it isn't. For instance, a recent national study found that while 65% of Americans self-identify as "Christian," about half of Americans believe people get to heaven through personal efforts. "A plurality of adults (48 percent) believe that if a person is generally good, or does enough good things during their life, they will "earn" a place in heaven."[7]

---

7. Carter, Joe, Joe Carter is a senior writer for The Gospel Coalition, Sarah Eek-hoff Zylstra, Justin Taylor, Phil Thompson • Andreas Köstenberger, Mike Minter,

Do you see the fallacy of that teaching? Paul knew better than that from personal experience. If anyone could get to heaven by doing good, Paul would have considered himself to be history's leading candidate. He told the Philippians that when it came to legalistic righteousness, he had been "blameless" (Philippians 3:4-6). Then he quickly added that he realized that all of his achievements had actually been meaningless. "But whatever gain I had, I counted as loss for the sake of Christ" (Philippians 3:7). What changed his mind?

Laser Beam Praying

On the road leading to Damascus, Syria, Paul was knocked to the ground by the appearance of Jesus Christ. After that encounter, Paul was a believer and a follower of Christ (Acts 9:1-19). In other words, he realized he needed grace, like every other sinner, in order to be saved. He needed to repent and turn to Jesus for salvation. He couldn't work his way to heaven; he needed to be saved.

When he prayed for his friends and family, therefore, he didn't pray that they would try harder or be better people. No. He prayed they would be saved. So when you pray for your friends and family, don't hesitate to pray as the Apostle Paul prayed. The main thing lost people need is salvation. Pray they will be saved!

A Christian friend of mine was a successful insurance salesman. In the early days of his career, he hesitated when asking for people to sign the contract. He didn't want to seem "pushy." Most of us can relate to that. One man, in particular, kept insisting that

---

Kevin DeYoung, et al. "Survey: Majority of American Christians Don't Believe the Gospel." The Gospel Coalition, August 9, 2020. https://www.thegospelcoalition .org/article/survey-a-majority-of-american-christians-dont-believe-the-gospel/.

someday he planned to buy a big life insurance policy from my friend. The man wanted to leave his family with the financial stability a life insurance policy could provide. My friend would ask him occasionally if he was ready to purchase the policy. Their conversations grew more and more relaxed, and their relationship as friends deepened, and my friend did not want to jeopardize their relationship by asking for a commitment. After all, the man kept promising, "someday, I'm going to buy that policy." So my friend never pushed.

One day the man suddenly died. My friend and his wife went to visit the widow, who had also become one of their closest friends. She told my friend she didn't know how she could go on without her beloved husband, but fortunately, he had provided for her and the kids. She thanked my friend for selling her late husband the life insurance policy since now, unfortunately, they were going to need it.

My friend felt like the room was going dark and was closing in on him when he had to look that grieving widow in the eye and admit he had never closed the deal. In spite of his convincing "sales pitch" to both the late husband and his widow, he had never pressed very hard to get her husband to sign the paperwork. Tragically, in spite of their close friendship and in spite of everyone's good intentions, there was no life insurance policy.

How does that true story relate to our prayer lives? Am I suggesting that evangelistic prayer is like selling insurance? No, not at all. What I am saying is that some things in life must be kept in laser-sharp focus. Some things are a matter of life and death. They can't take a back seat to lesser priorities, no matter how well-intentioned.

For years I kept a plaque on the wall of the church office. It simply read, "The main thing is to keep the main thing the main thing." When we pray for our lost friends, we may be tempted to remind God how sinful they are, how wrong they are, or how much their lives would improve if they would only change their ways. Or, because they mean so much to us, we may want to pray for them to have better jobs, better marriages, and a better quality of life. All of that is potentially good and helpful. There may be a hundred other blessings we may pray for them, with every prayer springing from our genuine concern for their well-being. But, in the final analysis, what good are temporary blessings if our lost friends and family are capable at any moment of slipping into eternity without Christ? Evangelistic prayer has to keep salvation as its primary focus.

So, in other words, when we pray, we need to "keep the main thing the main thing." We have no reason to hesitate when it comes to praying for lost people's salvation. Every other blessing, no matter how helpful and good it may be, is meaningful only for this short life but ultimately meaningless in light of the eternity our friends and families will face if they don't get saved. Leonard Ravenhill once said, "At the judgment seat, the most embarrassing thing the believer will face will be the smallness of his praying." With souls facing eternity, no wonder Paul's "heart's desire and prayer to God" was that "they may be saved." Why would we pray for less?

Prayer Prompts

- God, convict me that people without Christ are truly and permanently lost.
- Teach me to pray for the most important thing in lost people's lives—that they may be saved.

My Prayer List

List the people you are praying for and pray for them using the prompts above.

_____

_____

_____

CHAPTER 4

The Strategy
of Evangelistic
Intercession

*"First of all, then, I urge that supplications, prayers,
intercessions, and thanksgivings be made for all people,
for kings and all who are in high positions, that we may
lead a peaceful and quiet life, godly and dignified in
every way. This is good, and it is pleasing in the sight of
God our Savior, who desires all people to be saved and to
come to the knowledge of the truth."* —1 Timothy 2:1-4

You may never be more like Jesus than when you're praying for
other people. Why do I say that? Consider this: Jesus was born
of a virgin one time. He lived His sinless life one time. He died on
the cross one time. He rose from the dead one time. He ascended to
the Father one time. But ". . . He always lives to make intercession"
(Hebrews 7:25).

Intercessory prayer is the ministry of praying for other people. Intercession is so important Jesus now spends all His time interceding for His people. Knowing that Jesus prays for us stirs our faith. The influential 19th-century Scottish preacher Robert Murray McCheyne once wrote, "If I could hear Christ praying for me in the next room, I would not fear a million enemies. Yet distance makes no difference. He is praying for me." The commitment of Jesus to intercede on our behalf is a model for us to follow.

Intercession Ministry

Intercessory prayer has a rich biblical history, with examples from the lives of Abraham (Genesis 18), Moses (Exodus 33), and Samuel (1 Samuel 12), to name a few. Obviously, the early Church depended on intercession. Of course, as we have already observed, Jesus is our ultimate role model for intercessory prayer.

Why is intercessory prayer so crucial in God's plan? S. D. Gordon, the prolific American author of the late 19th and early 20th century, offers insight at this point. He said, "It helps greatly to remember that intercession is service: the chief service of a life on God's plan. It is unlike all other forms of service and superior to them in this: that it has fewer limitations. In all other services, we are constantly limited by space, bodily strength, equipment, material obstacles, and difficulties involved in the peculiar differences of personality. Prayer knows no such limitations."[8]

Put simply, intercessory prayer is a ministry on behalf of others with no natural restrictions. Prayer moves past objections and ignores arguments. Prayer relies on power that is greater than

8. Gordon, S. D. Essay. In *Quiet Talks on Prayer*, 13–13. Westwood, NJ: Christian Library, 1984.

the power of sinful man-made power structures, arguments, and human political reasoning. Prayer changes the spiritual climate. Intercession is one of God's main strategies for life change. Paul reminded Timothy that the ultimate aim of intercession for leaders is evangelism since God "desires all people to be saved."

That's why Paul instructed Timothy to pray and to intercede for leaders. Intercessory prayer is an essential evangelistic strategy. Paul knew Timothy would need to pray in order to make an evangelistic difference in his city. The same is true for us today.

Timothy had been assigned to pastor the church in Ephesus, a city mostly of ruins in modern-day Turkey. It was once a magnificent city, however, one of the largest in the Roman Empire. The edifice of the Library of Ephesus still stands today as a monument to its previous world-class status, where more than 12,000 volumes were housed during Timothy's pastoral tenure. There was also an astounding amphitheater in Ephesus, perhaps the largest in the ancient world, with a seating capacity of 24,000 people. They regularly gathered for sporting events and theater shows. Paul even once attempted to address the city from the ancient theater (Acts 19:29-41).

In Timothy's day, Ephesus was a seaport town, which allowed it to become one of the largest and wealthiest commercial centers in the ancient world. It was a capital city for Roman interests in Asia, with a population of about 200,000 people. As a result of its cosmopolitan demographic—with international travel occurring constantly, the city's sex traffic industry flourished with prostitution openly advertised and widely practiced.

Think of it. Ephesus was an entertainment, political, and commercial capital and a depraved metropolis with few rivals in the ancient world. Ephesus, like many similar cities in America, was a challenging place to plant a church, and intercessory prayer was a key part of Paul's evangelistic strategy. We could name multiple

American cities that fit the description of ancient Ephesus, and intercessory prayer is still a powerful weapon in the war on lostness today. How would that work?

Too often, believers in 21st-century America recognize a growing religious intolerance toward our faith. In fact, more than half of all Americans now believe religious liberty is declining in our country.[9] In the face of rapid cultural secularization, American Christians face challenges in our country not too dissimilar to the threats posed by the Roman Empire. Prayer, therefore, is still a powerful weapon in our spiritual arsenal. As Dick Eastman has correctly observed, "In no other way can the believer become as fully involved with God's work, especially the work of world evangelism, as in intercessory prayer."[10]

Our contemporary challenges are increasing. The deck, as the old saying goes, is stacked against us. But isn't that the way it always seems before a spiritual breakthrough occurs? How could the young, inexperienced Timothy hope to pierce the veil of spiritual darkness that hung heavy over Ephesus? Paul prescribed intercessory prayer. It has to be a part of our contemporary evangelistic strategy as well.

Power Prayer

There are seven nouns in the New Testament that describe prayer. Four of those appear in one verse:

9. Sullivan, Marissa. "Americans Believe Religious Liberty Is Declining, More Believe Christians Face Intolerance ." Lifeway Research, July 12, 2022. https://research.lifeway.com/2022/07/12/americans-believe-religious-liberty-is-declining-more-believe-christians-face-intolerance/.
10. Eastman, Dick. "Pg. 72." Essay. In *The Hour That Changes the World: A Practical Plan for Personal Prayer*. Grand Rapids, MI: Chosen Books, 2002.

"First of all, then, I urge that supplications,
prayers, intercessions, and thanksgivings be
made for all people." (1 Timothy 2:1)

Paul mentions *"supplications, prayers, intercessions, and thanks-givings."* Ironically, the one word translated, "intercessions," is rare and used nowhere else in the Greek New Testament. It seems to be, in this instance, a more inclusive word than merely praying for others. Instead of one word referring to intercessory prayer, actually, all four of the prayer words in this verse are focused on other people. In this case, therefore, all four words are essentially used to describe intercessory prayer. In verse 2, he identifies "kings and all who are in high positions" as the object of our intercession. Why?

Remember, Paul had just been released from prison prior to writing 1 Timothy. He personally understood the real political dangers of the new church in a major Roman city. His own ministry in Ephesus had been disrupted and essentially ended when authorities stepped in during the city riot involving Paul in Acts 19.

The Roman Empire could be a dangerous place for evangelistic Christians. Paul wanted Timothy to have every advantage and fewer disruptions while leading his evangelistic church in Ephesus. So, Paul urged him to pray for the people in power so that the Church could live "quiet lives." This probably meant that Christians should pray to be kept beneath the radar of Roman empirical scrutiny and intervention.

History demonstrates it is not always possible for the Church to avoid persecution, but it's worth praying for because God "desires all people to be saved and to come to the knowledge of the truth" (v. 4). Prayer for the authorities, therefore, was part of a larger, strategic evangelistic plan. Intercessory prayer is essential for those in authority because they have the temporal power to make our ministries either functional or frustrated. In reality, government overreach into our churches can disrupt our evangelism, discipleship, and our fundamental expressions of faith. That kind of government interference is unconstitutional for now, and in a democracy, we can vote, but we must also pray.

Just a few years before his death, Bill Bright, the late founder of one of the largest evangelistic ministries of the 20th century, wrote a discipleship guide on the subject of Christian citizenship. He listed prayer as the number one duty of a Christian citizen. Bright believed prayer is a priority for a Christian citizen in the United States because of evangelism.[11] Bright understood that as Christians, we are citizens of two kingdoms, yet ultimately our allegiance is not to a political party but to the King of Kings. Prayer for our nation, as a result, is never a passive action since prayer moves the hand that moves the world!

Our prayers for our nation, therefore, rise from our desire to keep government out of the free exercise of our faith, away from where and when we pray, how we choose to evangelize, or how we disciple our children. We sometimes need to pray to live "quiet lives" because God wants people all over our country to be saved, so we need the laws of our land to focus on something other than interfering in our historically protected constitutional freedoms of religion.

In the 20th century, for example, when communism threatened to snuff the fire of the gospel in Eastern Europe, a Dutch believer with a broken heart for Christians harassed by communist policies prayed for open doors. Smuggling Bibles and gospel tracts behind "the iron curtain" became his cause. Anne van der Bijl, known in the evangelical world by his code name, "Brother

11. Bright, Bill. Essay. In *Your 5 Duties as a Christian Citizen*, 3–3. Peachtree City, GA: New Life Resources, 2008.

Andrew," spent decades smuggling Bibles and gospel literature and was never arrested. He always prayed and taught others to pray, what came to be known as "the Prayer of God's Smuggler."

"Lord, in my luggage, I have Scripture that I want to take to your children across this border. When you were on Earth, you made blind eyes see. Now, I pray, make seeing eyes blind. Do not let the guards see those things you do not want them to see."[12]

One way or another praying for the governing authorities is a crucial part of evangelistic prayer, even if sometimes it means praying for them to leave us in peace to worship our God and practice our faith. For Christians in a hostile culture, we have one urgent issue—getting the gospel to the lost. If the Church draws undo attention to itself or becomes adversarial with the governing authorities over secondary issues, or if the Church becomes "the issue," it's harder for us to keep "the main thing the main thing." Perhaps that's one reason why Paul (remembering the riot in Ephesus that derailed his ministry there) urged Timothy to pray for the authorities so that "we can lead a peaceful and quiet life, godly and dignified in every way." We pray like this because God "desires all people to be saved."

---

12. Silliman, Daniel. "Died: Brother Andrew, Who Smuggled Bibles into Communist Countries." News & Reporting. *Christianity Today*, September 27, 2022. https://www.christianitytoday.com/news/2022/september/died-brother-andrew-open-door-smuggled-bibles-into-communis.html.

Prayer Prompts

- I will pray for these leaders so that the spread of the gospel can continue. I will pray their policies and decisions are godly and will not interfere with the spread of the gospel.
- I will pray for those in authority so that they govern with godly wisdom.
- I will pray for:

The President_____

My U.S. Senators

_____

_____

The Governor of my state

_____

The Mayor of my city

_____

Others

_____

_____

_____

My Prayer List

List the people you are praying for and pray for them using the prompts above.

_____

_____

_____

CHAPTER 5

Praying for Those
Who Evangelize

*"[Pray] also for me, that words may be given to
me in opening my mouth boldly to proclaim the
mystery of the gospel."* —Ephesians 6:19

*"Finally, brothers, pray for us, that the word of
the Lord may speed ahead and be honored, as
happened among you."* —2 Thessalonians 3:1

Do you like to ask for help? Researchers at the Harvard Business School found that an unwillingness to ask for help is one of the leading factors in feeling overwhelmed, but most people hesitate to ask for fear of looking weak or incompetent.[13] Asking, however, is not necessarily a sign of weakness.

---

13. "How to Get Better at Asking for Help at Work." Harvard Business Review, December 22, 2022. https://hbr.org/2022/12/how-to-get-better-at-asking-for-help-at-work.

The Apostle Paul is arguably the greatest Christian who ever lived, but his leadership status never stopped him from asking for prayer. Paul was a prayer warrior who depended upon prayer for every aspect of his ministry. In fact, Paul mentions prayer about 40 times—sometimes requesting prayer for himself but more often assuring his readers of his prayers for them (Romans 15:5-6; Romans 15:13; Ephesians 1:18; Ephesians 3:17-19; etc).

To the church at Ephesus, Paul appealed for prayer so that he would have the right words at the right time for evangelism. Think about that. When we read Ephesians, Romans, or any of his letters, does Paul ever seem at a loss for words? Isn't it the opposite? Do we not read his arguments with equal parts admiration for his skills of reasoning and communication, combined with enough confusion to humble us as he loses us in complex theological arguments and long, complicated sentences? Didn't the Apostle Peter acknowledge something close to the same when he wrote about Paul's communication skills and theological acumen? ". . . as he does in all his letters when he speaks in them of these matters. There are some things in them that are hard to understand, which the ignorant and unstable twist to their own destruction, as they do the other Scriptures." (2 Peter 3:16) Even Peter occasionally got momentarily lost in Paul's high soaring argumentation. Peter said that in all of Paul's letters, "some things in them . . . are hard to understand."

Paul clearly possessed a mastery of words. In fact, he was a cosmopolitan Roman citizen educated as the top student in the top rabbinical school in Jerusalem, and apparently, he was, by necessity, a highly proficient linguist specializing in Aramaic, Hebrew, Latin, and of course, Greek.

Yet, when it came to evangelism, Paul was dependent upon the prayers of the people he himself had led to Christ. He requested prayer from some of the very people he had taught to pray! Paul wanted to say the right things when it really mattered, so he asked the church to pray that the right words would come. Why?

Winning an Argument or a Soul?

Paul had discovered that there's a big difference between winning an argument and winning a soul. He had been full of arguments on the road outside the city walls of Damascus, Syria. His well-devised arguments were no match, however, for a blinding light from Heaven and the words of the resurrected Jesus, who confronted Paul in his own preferred language. Paul must have learned the significance of spiritual power over arguments while he was lying flat on his back in the road, unable to see a single glint of light in the middle of the day, with the words of Jesus ringing in his ears. After his encounter with Jesus, Paul readily testified, "my speech, and my message were not in plausible words of wisdom, but in demonstration of the Spirit, and of power" (1 Corinthians 2:4).

Paul knew all about constructing cunning arguments, but he turned his back on that approach in order instead to depend upon God's power. Fortunately, the same power at work in Paul can work through us. The only question is, "how do we get that power?" The answer is prayer.

Paul knew a secret about prayer and evangelism we all need to learn. Evangelism happens best when someone has been praying. In fact, it may be impossible to think of any evangelistic progress anywhere that wasn't preceded by prayer. The 19th-century American evangelist D. L. Moody once said, "Behind every work of God you'll always find some kneeling form." In other words, prayer always precedes salvation. Prayer, therefore, must always precede the mighty work of God in evangelism. So, in addition to praying for the lost person who needs to hear, we need to pray for the soul-winner who needs to speak!

This principle of praying for the evangelist is demonstrated repeatedly throughout history. For instance, it is widely known that Charles Spurgeon had a group of prayer warriors praying for people to be saved during each service at his church, the Metropolitan Tabernacle in London. The prayer team was in the basement of the church, in the "boiler room." There they prayed for people to be saved, but they also prayed for the preacher. Metropolitan Tabernacle was the largest evangelical church in the world at the time. In the years when Charles Spurgeon was pastor, thousands of people came to Christ. It was an evangelistic phenomenon in its day. Spurgeon himself regarded the "boiler room" as the secret of his church's massive growth and outreach.[14]

Another intriguing example of the importance of praying for the evangelistic preacher, teacher, worker, or soul-winner comes from American history before the time of Spurgeon. Charles G. Finley had been an attorney in New York in the early 1800s. He was saved at age 29 and was soon preaching around New York State and New England. His success in evangelism was immediate. Although he was criticized for his teaching and his methodology by some, Finley was, nevertheless, a man of prayer and greatly depended upon prayer for evangelistic results. His confidence in the power of prayer is probably most obvious when we look at his quiet, unassuming co-laborer and prayer partner. Daniel Nash, Finney's "intercessor" for seven years, made prayer the singular focus of his ministry.

---

14. "The Secrets of Spurgeon's Preaching: Christian History Magazine." Christian History Institute. Accessed March 15, 2023. https://christianhistoryinstitute.org/magazine/article/secrets-of-spurgeon.

Nash had previously served as a pastor who had devoted his life to intercessory prayer. He became Finney's associate with a single purpose—he prayed for the evangelist and the meetings where Finney preached. Nash would arrive in a community sometimes weeks before Finney was scheduled to speak. He would find the most committed prayer leaders in that community, and they would intercede for the power of God to fall upon Finney and the meetings. Nash and his teams would pray for days or weeks.

The significance of Nash's prayer ministry may be best understood by what occurred after his death in 1831. Finney's evangelistic ministry reached its "zenith" the same year. Almost immediately after Nash died, Charles Finney left the evangelistic ministry for a pastorate.[15] Nash died, and Finney's greatest days as an evangelist ended at the same time. The inference is clear. The prayer life of Daniel Nash was the secret of Charles Finney's success.

Nash's gravestone is a subtle tribute to his influence. It refers to his time as the evangelist's intercessor with this sparse statement: "Laborer with Finney, Mighty in Prayer." For some evangelistic Christians, few tributes could be better than this, "mighty in prayer."

Another example of the importance of interceding for those doing evangelism comes from the life of Pearle Goode. She was a widow in her early 60s in 1949 when Billy Graham was preaching in the big tent, sometimes called the "canvas cathedral" in Los Angeles, California. It was the success of that evangelistic "crusade" that helped propel the ministry of Billy Graham into legendary status in 20th-century America.

---

15. Johnson, James E. "Charles Grandison Finney: Father of American Revivalism." Christian History | Learn the History of Christianity; the Church. Christian History, October 1, 1988. https://www.christianitytoday.com/history/issues/issue-20/charles-grandison-finney-father-of-american-revivalism.html.

Many evangelicals know about the big tent in L.A., where Graham preached for weeks to upwards of 10,000 people per night. What is less well known is that there was a smaller tent nearby, where about 1,000 people were praying. The Lutheran evangelist Armin Gesswein, who was a prayer partner and mentor to the young Billy Graham, was leading the crusade prayer ministry. Every night 1,000 prayer warriors were kneeling in the tent, praying for the evangelist and for lost people to be saved.

One night, Pearl Goode, from nearby Pasadena, joined the prayer effort. There she found her calling. She poured her life into intercession for Billy Graham. After the Los Angeles crusade ended, she paid her own way to travel to American cities where Graham held more crusades. She privately rented hotel rooms near the crusades and prayed for Graham and for people to be saved. Eventually, the Graham organization learned about Pearl Goode's intercessory ministry, and they started bringing her to the cities.

When Goode died, Ruth Graham, the wife of the famous evangelist, attended the funeral. At the appropriate time, Mrs. Graham rose to speak and said, "Here lie the mortal remains of much of the secret of Bill's ministry."[16]

Billy Graham himself wrote of Goode's prayer life and its importance to his evangelistic ministry. His tribute was both personal and unusually candid about the supernatural aspect of intercession. "She prayed all night many nights, and I could sense the presence and power of that prayer. When she died, I felt it."[17]

---

16. Hartley, Fred A. Essay. In *Everything By Prayer*, 85–85. Revival Prayer Institute, 2012.

17. Batchelder, Christine. "Women's History Month: Pearl Goode." The Billy Graham Library, April 1, 2022. https://billygrahamlibrary.org/blog-womens-history-month-pearl-goode/.

Spurgeon's boiler room, Nash, the tent full of 1,000 intercessors in L.A., and Goode are all real versions of the same story. People interceding for evangelists and pastors make an incredible difference in the effectiveness of those ministries. Is it any wonder that Paul so frequently called for prayer?

So, since we know this, shouldn't all of us be interceding for the evangelistic leaders we know? What if every person reading these words decided to be their pastor's "Pearl Goode" or "Daniel Nash"? What if you went to your pastor and asked if you could organize a boiler room ministry at your church?

Prayer Prompts

- Pray for your pastor to be more effective in evangelism.
- Pray for your church staff to be more evangelistic.
- Pray that the members of your church would be more evangelistic.
- Pray that you and your family would be more evangelistic.
- Pray that your church will focus more on evangelism.

My Prayer List

List the people you are praying for and pray for them using the prompts above.

_____

_____

_____

CHAPTER 6

Shake It Up

"When they were released, they went to their friends and reported what the chief priests and the elders had said to them. And when they heard it, they lifted their voices together to God and said, "Sovereign Lord, who made the heaven and the earth and the sea and everything in them, who through the mouth of our father David, your servant, said by the Holy Spirit,

"'Why did the Gentiles rage,
*   and the peoples plot in vain?*
The kings of the earth set themselves,
*   and the rulers were gathered together,*
*   against the Lord and against his Anointed'*

for truly in this city there were gathered together against your holy servant Jesus, whom you anointed, both Herod and Pontius Pilate, along with the Gentiles and the peoples of Israel, to do whatever your hand and your plan had predestined to take place. And now, Lord, look upon their threats and grant to your

servants to continue to speak your word with all boldness, while you stretch out your hand to heal, and signs and wonders are performed through the name of your holy servant Jesus." And when they had prayed, the place in which they were gathered together was shaken, and they were all filled with the Holy Spirit and continued to speak the word of God with boldness."
—*Acts 4:23-31*

Earthquakes are awful. As I write these words, relief efforts are still underway following the major earthquakes in southeastern Turkey near the Syrian border, where, as of this writing, about 50,000 people have lost their lives. It has been one of the deadliest earthquakes of the 21st century.

It's true that big earthquakes ruin lives and cost unbelievable amounts of money, but even smaller, less destructive earthquakes can be unnerving. I grew up in Alaska, where earthquakes are more common than anywhere else in America. One hit Anchorage in 1964—the largest in American history—and seemed to almost swallow up the town. In my hometown of Fairbanks, I remember earthquakes that shook the house so hard dishes fell out of the cabinet, books bounced off the shelves, and everything in the house rattled and shook. My mother even resorted to hanging wind chimes inside the house. The chimes start clanging in response to mild tremors that human beings can't feel but that usually precede the big ones. It is a strange feeling to be in an earthquake because, for those few seconds, you are vulnerable to a power far outside your control.

For obvious reasons, the Bible often uses earthquakes in nature as a backdrop or a metaphor to display or explain the power of God. Familiar examples include the earthquake that occurred when Jesus died on the cross (Matthew 27:51-54). Another one shook the city as the tomb of Jesus was opened to reveal that His body had been raised (Matthew 28:2). Jesus predicted more earthquakes would occur as a sign of the impending end of time (Matthew 24:7). And, what Bible student could forget the earthquake that freed Paul and Silas from the stocks in the Philippian jail (Acts 16:25-26)? God has often used earthquakes, but none was any more impressive than the one that came as an answer to prayer! We will get to that in a moment.

Desperate Prayer

When the Church was in its infancy, problems seemed rare. The normal challenges of life were still present, of course, but everything had changed. Thousands of people had suddenly joined the previously tiny group. Miracles were occurring. People were experiencing the delirious joy of new life. God was moving in ways no one had ever seen before.

But, on the fringes of their excitement, challenges were lurking. They were about to need, and they were about to experience, the kind of powerful prayer which came to characterize the early Church in response to their challenges. First, however, they had to get desperate enough. They had to learn the biggest problems they ever faced were no match for God.

Problems drive us to prayer. Some of the greatest examples of prayer in Scripture sprang from a crisis or an emergency. Perhaps in your own life, you can remember a time when the urgency of your prayer was motivated by a child in the hospital, a fear of losing your job, a deadline you couldn't imagine meeting, or some immediate crisis. Is desperate prayer the wrong way to pray? Or is it part of God's design?

Leonard Ravenhill once made the bold statement, "God doesn't answer prayer-He answers desperate prayer." Perhaps Ravenhill was exercising some rhetorical hyperbole, but his point was clear. Our desperate situations lead us to pray with passion, a sense of urgency, and the realization that unless God hears and answers our prayer, our cause is lost. For instance, by his own admission, the late Timothy Keller had discovered a depth of prayer as a result of stage 4 pancreatic cancer, that he wouldn't trade for the prayer life he had pre-cancer. Knowing that the next scan could have revealed the cancer was out of control could leave anyone feeling a sense of desperation. Keller, the Christian author and founding pastor of Redeemer Presbyterian Church in New York City, called what he felt "scanxiety" every time he went for new scans for his cancer. As a result of the serious diagnosis and the natural feelings of dread, his prayer life had been unalterably deepened. He said, "This is going to sound like an exaggeration. My wife and I would never want to go back to the kind of prayer life and spiritual life we had before cancer, never."[18] Desperate circumstances can lead even trained theologians, pastors, and long-time devoted Christians to deeper dependence upon God through greater reliance upon the power of prayer.

The early Church found itself in exactly that kind of desperate situation. As a result, an earth-shaking, history-altering prayer meeting occurred. Their desperate problems drove them to desperate prayer. God was about to shake things up. The situation involved a man who was publicly healed, and the Apostles, Peter, and John, gave Jesus the credit. The miracle in Jesus' name excited opposition from the same religious leaders who, a few months

18. Quintanilla, Milton. "Tim Keller Gives Cancer Update, Says New Tumors 'Have Developed'." ChristianHeadlines.com. ChristianHeadlines.com, March 13, 2023. https://www.christianheadlines.com/contributors/milton-quintanilla /tim-keller-gives-cancer-update-says-new-tumors-have-developed.html.

earlier, had orchestrated the crucifixion of Jesus. The early persecution of the church was beginning.

The angry religious leaders detained Peter and John and forcefully threatened them not to speak publicly in Jesus' name again, releasing them with stern warnings to stop evangelizing (Acts 4:17-18). It may be tempting to underestimate the dilemma the early Church was in or the tension they felt. Although the timeline of events in Acts can be difficult to confirm with exactness, the arrest of the apostles probably occurred only a few months after Jesus had been arrested, tortured, and crucified. A few months, or as much as a year after the first arrest, the apostles would be arrested and imprisoned again, only to be freed by an angel. Almost immediately, they were rearrested, detained, threatened, and brutally beaten (Acts 5:18-40).

The climate surrounding the early Church was hostile and dangerous, and the religious establishment tried in every way possible to silence, imprison, or in some way suppress the Church. It was only going to get worse, and the Church leaders could probably see it coming.

The early Church was acutely aware of that environment of persecution when Peter and John were first arrested in Acts 4. The desperation of seeing their leaders arrested moved them to prayer (Acts 4:23-31). The result of their prayer was an earthquake that shook the place where they were praying (v. 31). More importantly, the church prayed until "they were all filled with the Holy Spirit and continued to speak the word of God with boldness" (v. 31). In other words, their desperation in prayer moved them to evangelize their city with the Holy Spirit's supernatural power, giving them boldness in their hostile culture.

Does this story resonate with us in 21st-century America? In some ways, it does. Church attendance is on the decline, atheism is on the rise, and most younger Americans, while being somewhat favorable toward the Bible, either believe it contains errors, or they have no opinion about it at all.[19] Most of us don't need a poll to know our culture is headed in the wrong direction spiritually, and as a result, we are praying for a much-needed revival.[20]

The question for those of us willing to pray and evangelize is this: are you willing to take a "wait and see" approach? If revival sweeps across the country, that would be a great development, but what if it delays? What if it doesn't happen? What if your lost friends and family members don't have long enough left if revival doesn't come? Will your sense of desperation to see them saved drive you to pray before it's too late?

The early Church didn't wait for a better time. Their desperate circumstances motivated them to take action in prayer. Will we recognize that desperate times call for desperate prayers?

Team Prayer

Before we leave this story of prayer, we have to accentuate one other feature of the early Church's prayerful evangelism. They prayed together (Acts 4:24). The language is clear, "they lifted their voices." The pronouns are plural. Their multiple "voices" are emphasized;

19. Chandler, Diana. "Teens Hold High View of Bible but Don't Read It Often, Barna Finds." Baptist Press. Accessed March 25, 2023. https://www .baptistpress.com/resource-library/news/teens-hold-high-view-of-bible-but-dont -read-it-often-barna-finds/.
20. Keller, Timothy. "American Christianity Is Due for a Revival." The Atlantic. Atlantic Media Company, February 5, 2023. https://www.theatlantic.com /ideas/archive/2023/02/christianity-secularization-america-renewal-modernity /672948/.

again, the word is plural. Then, in order to leave no doubt, Luke reminds us they lifted their voices "together." The prayer that reinvigorated the early Church to boldly evangelize in a hostile culture was not a lone voice calling in the wilderness. The prayer that re-lit the evangelistic fuse was a prayer meeting!

Why is this an important point? The book of Acts repeatedly shows that prayer meetings change the world. The early Church believed the evangelization of their city was important enough to justify gathering all the prayer warriors together to pray for evangelistic boldness.

The upper room in Acts tells us the same story. They were all gathered for prayer (Acts 1:14). When the answer came, 3,000 were saved (Acts 2:41). There are times when the most evangelistic praying occurs in a group, congregation, or even with a prayer partner or two.

I was at a local church in a prayer meeting recently with about 20 other leaders. On the wall of the prayer room was an old-fashioned black board with the names of lost people written in florescent chalk. That prayer room has groups of intercessors in and out all day, every day, praying for those lost people. The church believes that the souls of those people are valuable, and it is worth their time and effort to gather in teams and pray for the lost to be saved.

The New Testament advocates secret prayer, but it also teaches the importance of prayer meetings. You and I should regularly gather with others and pray for the lost to be saved and for the saved to be bolder, more disciplined, and more effective in evangelism. If you get desperate enough and join or organize a prayer group, you can make a difference. You can shake things up!

Prayer Prompts

- Pray for more desperation to pray for your lost friends to come to Christ.
- Pray for more desperation to share your faith with your lost family members.
- Seek God for a desire to organize a prayer group that prays for our lost friends to come to Christ.

My Prayer List

List the people you are praying for and pray for them using the prompts above.

_____

_____

_____

CHAPTER 7

Help Wanted!

*"And Jesus went throughout all the cities and villages,
teaching in their synagogues and proclaiming the gospel
of the kingdom, and healing every disease and every
affliction. When he saw the crowds, he had compassion
for them because they were harassed and helpless, like
sheep without a shepherd. Then he said to his disciples,
'The harvest is plentiful, but the laborers are few;
therefore, pray earnestly to the Lord of the harvest to send
out laborers into his harvest.'"* —Matthew 9:35-38

Are we running out of pastors? Some experts warn there's a pastoral shortage in the U.S.![21] Does it matter? More Protestant churches close than open, church members are twice as likely to be

---

21. Dash, Darryl. "The Coming Pastoral Shortage - the Gospel Coalition: Canada." The Gospel Coalition | Canada, February 15, 2023. https://ca.thegospelcoalition .org/columns/straight-paths/the-coming-pastoral-shortage/.

over 65 than the general population, and almost half of non-Christians have never had a conversation with a Christian about Christ.[22]

How can we evangelize America by depending upon an aging, dwindling clergy surrounded by more unchurched people and fewer churches? Is that really even the goal?

Think about it this way. There are about 380,000 churches in America.[23] Let's say; for argument's sake, each one has a pastor. About 60 percent of Americans self-identify as Christians in a U.S. population of about 332,000,000. Even if we were to assume that all of them are truly born again, that leaves approximately 132,000,000 unchurched, non-Christian Americans. So, in order to evangelize all of them through the clergy means, every pastor needs to personally evangelize about 348 individuals.

That all sounds possible—on paper—but, those statistics assume the best possible scenarios. In my own denomination (the SBC), once considered among the most evangelistic denominations, we have been in serious evangelistic decline for more than 20 years, hitting or hovering around record lows in evangelism year after year.[24] It's not just Southern Baptists, however, struggling to reach new people. With few exceptions, churches are not growing

---

22. Earls, Aaron. "22 Vital Stats for Ministry in 2022." Lifeway Research, January 11, 2022. https://research.lifeway.com/2022/01/05/22-vital-stats-for-ministry-in-2022/.

23. Goshay, Charita. "'Difficult Days Are Ahead' for America's Churches, Faith Institutions." *Akron Beacon Journal*, August 22, 2020. https://www.beaconjournal.com/story/news/local/2020/08/22/lsquodifficult-days-are-aheadrsquo-for-america rsquos-churches-faith-institutions/42282593/.

24. Cassidy, Captain. "2022 Annual Report: Another Bad Year for the Southern Baptist Convention." OnlySky Media, May 19, 2022. https://onlysky.media/ccassidy/2022-annual-report-another-bad-year-for-the-southern-baptist-convention/.

or successfully evangelizing in America. In fact, congregations and entire denominations are rapidly declining.[25]

So, is it reasonable to assume that less than half a million pastors, many nearing retirement age, are going to turn the sinking evangelistic ship around in the U.S.? No, it is not. In fact, the bigger question before us ought to be: Did Jesus even teach that we should rely upon paid clergy to evangelize America by themselves? The big issue related to evangelism is threefold: what are we supposed to do, are we doing it, and what should we do better?

The scope of the challenge is not decreasing. Jesus knew and taught that the harvest is potentially enormous. The size of the "prospect list," therefore, has never been the problem. Instead, Jesus said there weren't enough laborers in His harvest fields. In one of His most direct instructions regarding evangelistic prayer, Jesus made the appeal for a bigger workforce a main priority. He saw the evangelization of the nations through one lens: the need for more workers.

Then he said to his disciples, "The harvest is plentiful, but the laborers are few; therefore pray earnestly to the Lord of the harvest to send out laborers into his harvest." (Matthew 9:37-38).

From this little snapshot of a single event in one day in the life of Jesus, we learn a lot about evangelistic prayer.

A Big Harvest

Look what Jesus said, "The harvest is plentiful." When we pray, therefore, shouldn't we expect many people to be saved? Shouldn't

---

25. Gabbatt, Adam. "Losing Their Religion: Why Us Churches Are on the Decline." The Guardian, January 22, 2023. https://www.theguardian.com /us-news/2023/jan/22/us-churches-closing-religion-covid-christianity.

we pray for huge opportunities and massive evangelistic favor from God? Yes!

When I was a teenager, I went fishing in the Prince William Sound off the cold Pacific coast of Alaska with my uncle and one of his buddies. After fishing out on the open sea, at the end of a long day, my uncle lowered the anchor of his cabin cruiser near an inland cove not far from Valdez. I got out of the boat and walked along the gravel shoreline, and at a certain point, not far from our boat, I got an incredible surprise.

It was the time of year when salmon were swimming upstream. They instinctively return to spawn in the place where they were hatched. Apparently, an earthquake had altered the landscape because the stream they expected to swim into was inaccessible and visibly dry. The way forward was permanently blocked for the fish, so hundreds of big, beautiful salmon were swimming in one shallow pool of water, unable to continue any further. Once salmon start their strange upstream journey, they never retreat. So this huge swarming mass of big fish was swimming aimlessly in a relatively small cove of shallow water right in front of me. It was a bonanza of fish. Catching salmon that night was easy, and we baked two big ones on a small wood campfire and ate fresh salmon until we couldn't eat another bite. That's what "more than enough" looks like.

In a much more intense way and in an immeasurably more immense way, Jesus sees the evangelistic harvest somewhat like I saw that pool of salmon. The harvest is big. It's much bigger than we think. In light of His command, therefore, we have only one option. We should pray for many people to be evangelized and many more people than we've ever dreamed possible to be saved. "The harvest is plentiful."

Love the Lost

Jesus loves lost people. His instruction for us to pray for workers was preceded by a description of His "compassion." The word "compassion" in the original language describes an internal physical reaction. For Jesus, to see the unmet needs of people caused a visceral reaction. It's safe to say love was Christ's motivation for giving Himself sacrificially for sinners. The Bible says "For God so loved the world that He gave His only son . . ." (John 3:16). The Bible also says God proves His love for sinners by sending Jesus to die as a substitute for us (Romans 5:8). God's love for sinners moved Him to sacrificial action.

From His perspective, the lostness of those without Christ should incentivize us to pray for more workers. But does compassion motivate us to passionate prayer for more workers? Maybe not. Chuck Lawless, the evangelism professor, and author, recently said, "In my church consulting work, I cannot remember the last time I worked with a church who first prayed when they lacked workers. I've heard them complain. I've seen them establish committees. I've watched them develop worker enlistment campaigns. I've even encouraged them to do one-on-one recruiting. Most of these options may well have a place (except complaining, of course), but none has a place without prayer."[26]

The command of Jesus to pray for workers may be one of the most frequently disobeyed commands of Jesus. The bottom line is this; if we love lost people, we must pray for more evangelistic, godly influencers in their life. My children are all adults now,

---

26. Lawless, Chuck. "10/09/18 Praying for Laborers." ChuckLawless.com, October 9, 208. https://chucklawless.com/2018/10/10-09-18-praying-for-laborers/.

but all of their lives, I've prayed for them every day. One of my most frequent prayers is that God will place other godly influencers around them.

My children are Christians, but I still want them surrounded by godly influencers, whether they're in school, at work, in relationships, on vacation, or wherever they may be. When we are praying for lost people, it should be the same. We pray for them to be saved, and of course, we also ask God how we can witness to them, but in addition, one of the most powerful prayers we can pray is for our lost friends to be surrounded by godly influencers. Ask God to place the other laborers Jesus referred to into their lives. Other voices, in addition to our own, speaking into their lives greatly enhances the evangelistic process. Love for our lost family members and friends motivates us to pray, "send more workers."

Passionate Prayer

Most Bible translations do not include the word "earnestly" when describing the kind of praying we do for more laborers in the evangelistic harvest. The word is an editorial choice, however, by the ESV translators. Why? Perhaps the word is implied since the verb "pray" is based on a grammatical form in the Greek New Testament emphasizing urgency. No Greek verb form expresses a more immediate action. In fact, the form of the verb "pray" could be translated literally as "pray immediately!" Or, perhaps the Greek word translated "pray" explains the use of the word "earnestly." There are multiple words in the New Testament for "pray." The one in Matthew 9:38 means, at its root, "to lack." It usually carries the idea of a desperately needed gift, blessing, or favor. The root word means "to lack, to be in need, or to want." As a word for prayer, it always conveys a desperate need for something desired which needs to be supplied or provided. The picture is one of coming empty-handed, seeking what God can provide. It is the word that conveys "pleading" in prayer.

Imagine having that kind of passion as you pray for more soul winners, witnesses, or evangelists to be raised up in your church or your nation. If Jesus commands us to pray it, God is ready to answer it!

If you've been attending church for long, you'll start to notice during those early summer Sundays, the children's minister starts getting creative, passionate, and desperate when it comes to finding Vacation Bible School workers. They need teachers, teenagers to help with recreation, creatives to build props, small groups to donate snacks, and retired guys to direct traffic. The entire church is recruited.

Now ask yourself, what if our prayer meetings were filled with that same kind of urgency to pray for more evangelists, pastors, and witnesses for Christ? Have you ever sensed that kind of urgency in prayer for more evangelistic workers?

Jesus sees the need in our towns and cities just like He did 2,000 years ago. He's still commanding us to pray for more workers. Will you do it?

Prayer Prompts

- Pray that the Lord would give you a big vision of the big potential in evangelism.
- Pray that godly influencers would befriend your lost family members and friends and witness to them.
- Pray for a passion to pray for more evangelistic workers to arise in your church and your nation.

My Prayer List

List the people you are praying for and pray for them using the prompts above.

_____

_____

_____

CHAPTER 8

Praying for the Power

"And while staying with them, he ordered them not to depart from Jerusalem but to wait for the promise of the Father, which, he said, 'you heard from me; for John baptized with water, but you will be baptized with the Holy Spirit not many days from now.'"

"So when they had come together, they asked him, "Lord, will you at this time restore the kingdom to Israel?" He said to them, "It is not for you to know times or seasons that the Father has fixed by his own authority. But you will receive power when the Holy Spirit has come upon you, and you will be my witnesses in Jerusalem and in all Judea and Samaria, and to the end of the earth." —Acts 1:4-8

How significant is the right kind of power at the right time? I'm from Alaska, so I've experienced some freezing temperatures, but I'm not a fan of cold weather. Today I live in central Texas, where winters are usually mild. In February 2021, however, a historic winter storm put Texas in a deep freeze for days. It was a winter no one expected and few Lone Star State residents had ever experienced. It was one for the record books.

The biggest problem that winter was a lack of power. The electric demands were unprecedented as Texans needed to heat their homes. For the first time in history, all 254 Texas counties were under a winter storm warning at the same time. The financial losses due to storm damages climbed into the billions. More than 200 people died. It was serious. As a result of the high demand for electricity, most of us experienced some power failure. Some homes were without electricity for days. Since then, we've heard a lot of discussion regarding the electric grid and the state's preparedness for future winter freezes. Obviously, no one wants to experience a massive loss of power again.[27]

We rely on power for every aspect of modern life. What is a dishwasher, for instance, when the electricity or water is turned off? Or, what use does a car serve if it's out of gas or a cell phone when it has a dead battery? Almost everything in our lives functions properly when it is connected to power, and yet it's all practically useless when it's not connected to power. The Christian life is designed the same way—we thrive when we're connected to the Spirit's power, and we flounder when we're not. In no other area of our Christian lives is that more true than when we attempt to evangelize. Power makes all the difference.

---

27. Oberholtz, Chris. "On This Day: The Great Texas Freeze Began and Would Rank among Worst Winter Storms in History." Fox Weather. Fox Weather, February 10, 2023. https://www.foxweather.com/weather-news/7-facts-from -great-texas-freeze.

As we have already observed in a previous chapter, Jesus initially prohibited His disciples from rushing into the city with news of His resurrection. Instead, after the resurrection, He spent 40 days training them in matters related to the Kingdom of God (Acts 1:3). Surprisingly, after about three years of personal discipleship with Jesus as their instructor and a 40-day intensive with Him after He defeated death, they still weren't ready to tell the story. They had a power problem. On the surface, most of us would have assumed they were ready to go, but looks can be deceiving.

When Tina and I got married, we were broke, but we both had jobs a few miles apart from each other. My dad had gone out of town and left me his Cadillac to drive, so I decided to meet Tina for lunch. Dad's Cadillac was new, with a baby blue metallic exterior, a white leather roof, and brilliant chrome wheels. I was cruising down the main street of my hometown in a new Cadillac, feeling like a million bucks! Except, I was broke and almost out of gas. Tina had cash, so I was hoping to make it to her job for gas and lunch money. I only had a one-dollar bill that day. Unfortunately, I ran out of gas, on the main street of my hometown, on a beautiful sunny day, during a busy lunch hour, in a baby blue Cadillac. But it got worse. The gas station was less than a block away and downhill. So I got out and started pushing the Cadillac to the gas station.

Trying to do evangelism apart from the power of the Holy Spirit is somewhat like pushing a brand new Cadillac into a gas station—both propositions represent a vivid and absurd display of powerlessness. Each circumstance is a public reminder that without power, we're totally ineffective. A church, or an individual believer, can appear to be well equipped and even impressive, but like a new Cadillac with an empty tank, there's no progress, and we push when we should be driving. Just like my dad's car, however, we were made for power. We were made to go, but we are powered by a source outside ourselves. We can't generate that power on our own, no matter how hard we try.

The Promise of Power

Before Jesus entrusted the disciples with the task of world evangelization, He urged them to wait for the power of the Holy Spirit. He apparently expected nothing from them in the beginning except prayer. Before He ascended, Jesus made it very clear what He expected and what was at stake.

"And while staying with them, he ordered them not to depart from Jerusalem, but to wait for the promise of the Father, which, he said, "you heard from me; for John baptized with water, but you will be baptized with the Holy Spirit not many days from now" (Acts 1:4-5).

The disciples had the propensity to misunderstand, so not unlike us, they missed the larger point and immediately quizzed Jesus about current political matters (Acts 1:6-7). Jesus corrected their obsession with national politics and reminded them of the global scale of their calling:

> "But you will receive power when the Holy Spirit has come
> upon you, and you will be my witnesses in Jerusalem and
> in all Judea and Samaria, and to the end of the earth."
> (Acts 1:8)

The disciples then spent the time between when Jesus promised the power and when the outpouring of the power actually occurred, in night and day prayer (Luke 24:53; Acts 1:12-14). They knew they were waiting in worship, praise, and prayer for the outpouring of the Holy Spirit, but they didn't know when or how the power would come. All they could do was pray. Pentecost, and all of the Holy Spirit power that came with it, was the answer to their prayer!

From their experience, we discover some principles for evangelistic ministry. For one thing, we need the Holy Spirit's power to effectively evangelize. For another thing, prayer has always attracted the Spirit to a person, a church, or a movement. So if we want the anointing of the Holy Spirit, we need to pray!

The Examples

Not only does Scripture teach the importance of prayer to receive the Spirit's power, but we also have powerful examples from history. For instance, D. L. Moody was the pastor of a large church in 19th-century Chicago when he began feeling as if there was no power in his life. Prompted by two godly women in his congregation, he started praying for the power of the Holy Spirit. Then it happened. While walking through New York City, praying for the power of God, the Spirit filled him.

Of the experience, he wrote, "One day, in the city of New York—oh, what a day!—I cannot describe it, I seldom refer to it; it is almost too sacred an experience to name. . . . I can only say that God revealed himself to me, and I had such an experience of his love that I had to ask him to stay his hand. I went to preaching again. The sermons were not different; I did not present any new truths, and yet hundreds were converted. I would not now be placed back where I was before that blessed experience if you should give me all the world—it would be small dust in the balance."[28] The principles to glean from Moody's experience should be obvious. He prayed for

---

28. "Dwight L. Moody Turns 172." Desiring God, April 24, 2023. https://www.desiringgod.org/articles/dwight-l-moody-turns-172.

the power of the Holy Spirit, and when he experienced the anointing, he led more people to Christ. There is a direct relationship between prayer, the Spirit, and evangelistic results.

The backstory of Billy Graham's legendary evangelistic success is similar. While a young Graham was in London just after WW2, he heard Stephen Olford preach on the subject of the Spirit-filled life. Graham would later call Olford the man who had most influenced his ministry.[29] After he heard Olford preach, Graham confessed to him that he needed to be filled with the Spirit—that he knew his ministry lacked the Spirit-filled life that Olford was describing.

"One day, decades later, I had lunch with Stephen Olford, and he told me the story in detail regarding what happened after that first introduction to Billy Graham. The two men met in Pontypridd in the South of Wales, where they fasted and prayed for two days. Olford taught Billy Graham what Scripture says about the Holy Spirit, and Graham cried out to God for the Spirit's anointing. On the second day of prayer and fasting, Billy Graham jumped to his feet, clapped his hands, and praised God that he had been filled with the Spirit.

The two men agreed to meet after Graham preached that night at a youth event. When Olford arrived, the parking lot was jam-packed. Graham was already preaching. Olford told me that the atmosphere was electric. He could tell that something was different. Before Dr. Graham finished preaching, young people were already leaving their seats and crowding to the front, giving their lives to

29. "Olford Ministries Continues to Influence the World." Olford Ministries Continues to Influence the World - Memphis Daily News. Accessed April 25, 2023. https://www.memphisdailynews.com/news/2018/mar/20/olford-ministries-continues-to-influence-the-world/print.

Christ. Later that night, Stephen Olford told his father, regarding Billy Graham, "The world will hear from that young man."

In Scripture and in experience, seeking the Spirit's power and anointing precedes greater effectiveness in evangelism. If we are going to pray effectively for evangelism and it's positive, saving results, we must pray for ourselves and others to be filled with the Holy Spirit.

An evangelism professor and author, Tim Beougher, recently said it succinctly. "The power for evangelism is the Holy Spirit. We must be filled and empowered by the Holy Spirit as we witness."[30] I couldn't have said it better!

Prayer Prompts

Lord, I believe you want me to be Spirit filled

_____

Lord, I believe you want me to evangelize in the power of the Holy

Spirit _____

Father, fill me with the Holy Spirit _____

30. "The Power of Evangelism: The Holy Spirit: Ministry: Kregel Academic and Ministry." Kregel Academic and Ministry | Faithful books engaged with the academy and culture, July 23, 2021. https://kregelacademicblog.com/ministry /the-power-of-evangelism-the-holy-spirit/.

My Prayer List

List the people you are praying for and pray for them using the prompts above.

_____

_____

_____

EPILOGUE

We all know people who need Jesus. They may be in our family, our neighbors, co-workers, or friends. Regardless of how they relate to us, people need to hear the gospel and be given an opportunity to respond to it. Evangelistic prayer prepares the way for the gospel to be shared and received.

The need is greater now than ever. Lostness is increasing faster than we are evangelizing.

Prayer for the lost is talked about everywhere, but the biggest problem we face is not unanswered prayer. The biggest problem is unoffered prayer.

Imagine what could happen if Christians took prayer as seriously today as the early Church did in the book of Acts. How long do you think it would take before we experienced revival and spiritual awakening?

It is up to you now. We have studied approaches to evangelistic prayer in this book. But we need to make evangelistic prayer a regular part of our life.

Here are some practical ways to make praying for the lost a part of your daily prayer life.

Let's start with an extremely personal question: Have you made the commitment to pray daily?

In the most famous teaching on prayer in history, Jesus instructed us to pray for our "daily bread" (Matthew 6:11). We can only pray for daily bread if we are praying every day. It is God's will for every believer to seek Him on a daily basis. The most important decision you can make as a believer is the decision to personally seek God every day. Every aspect of your Christian life will be affected by that deliberate choice.

How to Pray Daily

Decide when you will pray. Decide where you will pray. Then, commit and do not stop. If you miss a day, start over. Your success in prayer will come down to some fundamentals you intentionally choose to repeat daily, for as long as you live, to the glory of God.

If you do not have a set time for prayer and a set place for prayer, you will not have a consistent prayer life. Jesus said, "But when you pray, go into your room, and shut the door and pray to your Father who is in secret. And your Father who sees in secret will reward you" (Matthew 6:6). Without consistency and commitment, we find plenty of excuses not to pray. If we have a commitment to meet God every day and a plan for how to keep the commitment and a time and place set aside, excuses melt in the face of resolve.

If our prayer lives are inconsistent, we are missing something. The blessing of God or what Jesus called the "reward" is promised to those who meet with Him in daily prayer in the personal place of prayer (v. 6).

What difference does it make if we pray every day? Most importantly, Jesus expects it. Additionally, something of eternal significance is at stake when we pray. The souls of those we could be praying into the kingdom are in the balance! In other words, other people's spiritual lives are an important reason why we need to pray daily. Intercessory prayer is powerful prayer.

One of the most unsettling passages of Scripture found in the Bible concerns the lack of intercession. Ezekiel 22:30 teaches that

God works through and looks for intercessors who will pray for souls to be saved, because God wants to show His mercy to sinners! "And I sought for a man among them who should build up the wall and stand in the breach before me for the land, that I should not destroy it, but I found none."

Our prayers are more than well-meaning sentimental gestures. Our prayers are more than a way for us to experience peace of mind. Our prayers outlast our own lives. Our prayers change destinies. Our prayers affect eternity.

On my daily prayer list I have people listed who need Jesus. I never want to miss an opportunity to pray that today could be the day they receive Christ.

Prayer Lists

Keeping a prayer list can help you pray every day! Some people may find a prayer list to be too mechanical and lacking spontaneity, but prayer is both devotion and discipline. Prayer rises easily from the devotional warmth of our deep concern for the lost, but some days we are not at our best. Some days we do not feel like praying (those are the days we need prayer the most). When the feelings of devotion are lacking, discipline and a commitment to prayer need to kick in. That is one way we pray without ceasing (1 Thessalonians 5:16). We decide to abide!

Prayer lists can always help, but especially on the days when our minds are wandering, our hearts are distracted, and our schedules threaten to disrupt our time alone with God. Write down your prayer request and review it often.

I urge you to keep a prayer notebook close by and use it daily. It can be as simple as an old-fashioned spiral notebook, or you can use a popular blank-sheet journal that are readily available. I have tried various methods to find what works best. For the past few years, I simply designed and printed my own and put the daily pages in a ring binder. Or, maybe better yet, yours is electronic on your phone, tablet, or computer. There are plenty of great options, as long as it is something that works for you, and you will stick with it.

Whatever you choose, make a list of the specific people you are praying for every day (the people you wrote down in this book, plus maybe others the Lord brings to your mind). Choose one of the Scripture promises found in this book and write it next to their name. Pray that promise every day for the people on your list.

You could start by choosing one person you know who needs to be saved. Put their name on your prayer list and pray for them every day. Or list seven people you know who need Jesus. Write out their names—one for each day of the week. Select a Scripture promise and write it near their name. Pray for a different person each day for a week and keep praying until they meet Jesus! Prayer will make a difference.

Prayer Cards

A short stack of seven prayer cards might work better for you than keeping a list. Even something the size of a credit card can work well. Write your friend's name on one side of the blank card and the Scripture promise on the other side. Keep them close by. Or make two or three identical sets—leave them where you know you will be spending time each day. For instance, make one set for your desk, one for your bathroom mirror, and one for your pocket or purse.

However you use the prayer cards, the idea is to pray for people who need the Lord. God hears our prayers when we are interceding. We may even resemble Jesus most when we pray for others, "since He always lives to make intercession for them" (Hebrews 7:25).

Small Groups

In the four gospels we rarely see anyone praying except Jesus, and He often prayed alone. The book of Acts, however, introduces a prayer model we see throughout the rest of the New Testament. When we read about people praying in Acts and throughout the epistles, they are frequently praying with other people. Prayer meetings—no matter how large or small—change the world. With that in mind, where could you join a group who would pray with you?

Your church small group might be the best place to pray for the lost. Your group may use different books to study periodically, or you might rely upon a pre-determined curriculum for your Bible study. Why not suggest an eight-week mini-series with this book or add it as a supplement, and get your entire small group focused on evangelism? Your group can brainstorm together on powerful ways to pray for the lost so more people can be saved.

Remember, the upper room in the book of Acts was a small group who prayed together for ten days, and the result was Pentecost with three thousand conversions in a single day. The New Testament makes it clear that God loves it when groups of believers pray together for a common result. Regardless of what group you lead or join, praying with others for the lost is a biblical model that brings about incredible results.

A Co-Mission

When Jesus appeared to His disciples after the resurrection, He gave them (and us) what we call the Great Commission. Hear what He said, "Go therefore and make disciples of all nations, baptizing them in the name of the Father and of the Son and of the Holy Spirit, teaching them to observe all that I have commanded you. And behold, I am with you always, to the end of the age" (Matthew 28:19-20).

For more than three hundred years, missionaries have referred to the Matthew 28 passage as the Great Commission because it is a "co-mission" between God and us. He sends us to the lost, and we go and share the gospel. When it comes to praying evangelistic prayers, one of the things we pray actually involves us.

How can God use you to share the gospel with the people you are praying for? Prayer is powerful, but eventually someone must explain the gospel in a way lost people can understand it. You can be the answer to your own prayer. Ask God to give you the faith to step out of fear and tell your family members and friends about Jesus. Be like the prophet Isaiah who prayed, "Send me" (Isaiah 6:8).

Be Creative

There are many other ways to stay motivated to pray daily for people to be saved. Spend some time thinking of a way or ways that fit your personality. Whatever God leads you to do to make evangelistic prayer a daily activity is a good thing. Pray now for the Spirit to give you insight into how you can make evangelistic prayer a part of your life.

Finally, once you start praying evangelistic prayers, start recruiting your Christian brothers and sisters to do the same. Help us spread the news about evangelistic prayer!